D0970972

Only Ride
Copyright © 2014 by Megan Volpert

Cover art courtesy of Wikimedia Commons

Cover design by Mona Z. Kraculdy

Sibling Rivalry Press, LLC
13913 Magnolia Glen Drive
Alexander, AR 72002

info@siblingrivalrypress.com

www.siblingrivalrypress.com

ISBN: 978-1-937420-61-1

Library of Congress Control Number: 2013956734

First Sibling Rivalry Press Edition, March 2014

ONLY RIDE

MEGAN VOLPERT

SIBLING RIVALRY PRESS
Alexander, Arkansas
www.siblingrivalrypress.com

I don't believe the good times are over.
I don't believe the thrill is all gone.
Real love is a man's salvation.
The weak ones fall; the strong carry on.

Tom Petty, "Straight Into Darkness"

ONLY RIDE

FOR MINDY

Only idiots ride into the sunset

It's all very well & romantic from the perspective of those left behind, a silhouette charging forth against the great orange beyond. But if you're the lucky bastard sitting on that iron horse, it's an investment in blindness. Put mirrors over your eyes, or view the road trip from behind a rose-tinted face shield. Or turn your back on the big yellow metaphor & give no quarter to sentiment. I don't know the precise moment when I first looked upon my own mortality with respect. There was blood on it. This is a story that takes place in the black, but it need not happen at night.

VOLPERT

We are not precious little boats

There are a half dozen things I associate with f-holes &
each of them is a god you have never met. Everything is
a time capsule in which we are born back ceaselessly,
if ceaselessly actually means occasionally. No matter
how steadily one keeps a hangover in the crosshairs,
the mind is not a sieve. Memory is a shiv, happening
pointedly poignantly, like a house on fire. It doesn't
matter how prepared you are to carry possessions out
safely. Ash is a part of the air. So the fearsome thing
really is life. That's why we breathe deeply & live it,
wiggling our loose teeth with our wagging tongues.

VOLPERT

The inferno is cool

There's getting fucked up, being fucked up & feeling fucked up. You get it at the bar, you be it at work & you feel it in writing. We have to choose between the do not disturb hanger & the room service breakfast hanger. Generally I ask to be left alone, but in the parlance of our times, I do aspire to be the purveyor of an innovative document solution for this communication challenge. The trouble is that my few heroes are all semi-rotten bastards. Most of my students write their role model paper about Mommy, Daddy & Jesus. I just never would've done that.

VOLPERT

I never asked for a pony

My parents have always been terrible gift givers. It was many years before I noticed, because they largely kept to my childhood lists. The divorce ended their system of checks & balances, replacing it with a competition for the affection that in adulthood I have granted begrudgingly at best. My mother exhausts whole rolls of cellophane tape on bric-a-brac packages containing frog motifs or wild west themes. My father never sends a note with playing cards, old-fashioned candy & stuffed animals won out of the claw game during bowling league. Either they do not suspect my ingratitude, or they do not wish to address it.

VOLPERT

These are the kingdom's keys

ONLY RIDE

My father used to carry an entire pack of black Bic ultra fine points in his back pants pocket. He would take one out to sign our permission slips, but we could never borrow them. He guarded these pens & I would sometimes have to go into another room just to retrieve one of the cheap ballpoints we got for school. In junior high, I took a drafting class & learned to mimic my father's precision penmanship, also ferreted away a bit of lunch money to buy myself his better instruments. Given the opportunity to steal any of his pens, I certainly did so every time.

VOLPERT

Cut the crusts off

My mother argued that all the vitamins were in the crust, but this was before you could whip out a phone & verify stuff. She said deli sandwiches & my father said lunch meat, even if it was for dinner. My mother did the best she could with the names of things. She was on an Easter egg hunt, sweeping through increasingly improbable places for the good nugget. My father could eat an entire angel-food cake in one sitting. I never saw him eat chocolate, just like I never saw him wear shorts. He was more of a piñata type, deeply bashing away at one thing.

VOLPERT

There are no guns in my house

My father used to take me to the fair to play shoot out the star & win a prize, just with BBs. It was hard to score that rubber chicken, but I got about six of them over the years. He taught me to think about how many shots to drop it, how many to make the red middle fall out & where. A child is not like those stars. It would make sense to aim for the self-esteem, to poke holes in the accomplishments. A child will stand there in the sight line, melting away with each round. Paper stars have more resistance.

VOLPERT

Get in a position to argue

Right on the edge of his chair, weight on the balls of his feet, my father would be ready to spring a pointed finger at me to punctuate the yelling. After a decade of work on debate teams, I understand that the quickest route to a win is to appear relaxed. Slack your jaw & slouch a little. Tense only the unseen muscles. Tighten your asshole & limit your attention. Don't listen to the opposition too well, or you will often accidentally agree with it. Better that your mind will develop a heart of its own, secreting the mortar with which you will fortify your mansion of glory.

There are always latex gloves
in my kitchen

I remember standing over my father, dozing & wheezing in his La-Z-Boy, a butcher knife in my hand. Warned myself a hundred times to be sure it doesn't get caught on the ribs. This is a false fantasy repeatedly brought to my surface while doing a week's worth of nasty dishes as a teenager. When the thumb in one glove got leaky, I'd trap a roach in a dirty cup to try to guilt my mother into spending $2.99 on a new pair, then flush the roach alive down the toilet. My father never laid a hand on me, but the man could yell for hours at a time. He was always saying he'd squash you like the bug that you are.

VOLPERT

A blindfolded chimpanzee
on crack could do this

That's what Coach Eden said when I turned in my slapdash volleyball remediation packet after being out sick with mono for two months during sophomore year. Granted, I was the bitchy girl who smoked cigarettes in the bathroom before school & led others in a walking revolt during the mile run. This woman sharpened her irrelevance into a demeaning pinprick on the surface of my inflatable universe. There is a scar on my knee. Eden tried to make an example of me during a tennis demo. I dove hard & killed it back on her feet. The hypothetical monkey would most likely have applauded this alongside the other eighty girls.

VOLPERT

Fortune favors the fortunate

One Sunday night I came home because of school the next morning & when I opened the screen door it was busted. My father grounded me for two weeks for that broken latch, even though I hadn't been around in three days to do it. He said that was fine, but I could stay grounded for whatever else I hadn't yet done. If I had the ability to tell the future, I wouldn't play the lotto or anything. I'd just go to the store & pick up milk before it rains, or tell my friends to set a battery powered alarm clock so they don't oversleep during the blackout.

VOLPERT

We didn't escape in cars at night

I discovered the small muscles that keep a shoulder together when we began buying beater cars from police auctions. These were long-nosed rusty animals with heavy doors that had to be slammed to stay shut, running a few months then laid to rest while my father worked up to admitting each defeat. He spent weekends with his head under the hood. I learned all the local bus routes & protocol for hitching rides. None of us four kids got a driver's license when we turned sixteen & I didn't take an interest in Springsteen until I was almost thirty.

VOLPERT

Everybody sings in the shower

One summer in high school I briefly knew how to play that Violent Femmes song on guitar. I was at debate camp & the guy who taught it to me could also stick a dime up his nose, then cough it out his mouth. Everybody can do that, but most people don't try. We always let him keep the dime. Now, there is the dream where one light blue wall of my office boasts an unstrung black Fender Stratocaster. Air guitar is on my mind lately, filed next to 2% milk as a thing for children & adults who occasionally indulge in mildly reckless behavior.

VOLPERT

We all fight

I think it would be cool to own a switchblade. But that means carrying it around & then that means using it, which seems like no fun. I'm not a violent person. Go ahead & throw me under the bus though, because I can lift it with my tongue. No kid ever bullied me in school. For years, I didn't understand it was because of my smart mouth. I didn't even know I had one until my father put soap in it. All people are strong & most don't know what their strengths are. The life is perfectly salvageable. It's just the person is not yet interested in getting saved.

VOLPERT

We are random number generated

Not knowing the tiny cinema in Ann Arbor was an independent theater, I stood looking at the posters in the lobby & thinking I was just out of it in terms of currently running movies. Everything showing at this indy place appeared utterly mainstream. Imagine being that kind of kid, so open that subtitles & cult underground queers could feel completely normal. I only realized later that I had inadvertently done something cool. And I was so cool, I hadn't even noticed that I was that cool. Hannibal Lecter said the first step in the development of good taste is to credit one's own opinion.

VOLPERT

There's a last time for everything

Senior year, I dated an exchange student & her boyfriend. Silver skulls capped his car door locks & he was the dreamiest pothead who had graduated the year before. We would go to the lake & smoke cigarettes in sand, dodging the cops' flashlights after curfew. She went back to Berlin & he became day-shift assistant manager at Jewel-Osco. He mumbled something about community college, bagged my groceries when I came home for winter break. I asked him about the Chevelle. He'd traded it for a Thunderbird. Neither of us knew how to spell her last name, so we didn't keep in touch with her.

VOLPERT

Changes come around

I told myself to remember an Egyptian girl on the bus riding past a Christmas tree lot & still carry it, without meaning & whether it ever had any. This was a time when people across America wore loose-fitting clothing. In this same era, I was thin & I wish I had known it at the time. What I don't know now is the last name of that bitch who stole my first high school boyfriend, or the last time I paid full price for anything. But on the highway with my mother when I was sixteen, we sang John Cougar's instructions at the top of our lungs.

VOLPERT

Everything still turns to gold

This is back in senior year the first time I read that book about the island & I'm likely being romantic but I think we just finished the chapter where Simon dies. In the afternoon moving up the stairwell from English to Econ, if there was sun it was poised right in that tall window. The blond banister was warm that day as I pulled myself up & everything had a shine on it. High school & I were not kind to each other. If I ever go back there it will be to sit on that middle step waiting for the light to pass through.

I'm not Velma

There are concave people & convex people. Everyone walks either tits first or shoulders first. I walk shoulders first, like a cross between a bird & a yeti. In high school, a few people nicknamed me Shaggy. After graduation, you don't mess with people who walk with their shoulders out front. I had my midlife crisis at eighteen because it seemed highly unlikely I would live past thirty. But here I am now, not knowing what to do with the mysterious fact that I am the same older age as Britney Spears, who walks tits first like the bird in her chest wants out.

VOLPERT

I'm skipping the reunion

Most of the girls I dated when I was growing up are still moving on to dudes with nice personalities or good dope. It's true that I don't always say or do the right things, but my wife puts up with me every time because that's what marriage means. We are always trying to be better, to be the same people we fell in love with & at the same time to be new people who are way more awesome. I'm not trying to sound uplifting, or even to rub it in. Proof is not required. It's just that I'm not sorry for being happy.

VOLPERT

To each her own lobotomy

I lived with this girl who didn't ever want me to keep any white wine in the house. Her mother was an alcoholic. Specifically, she kept two boxes of white wine in the fridge at all times. I didn't want it from the box, but sometimes during the summer you just get a hankering for that dry sweetness in the glass. When she moved out, I drank nothing but white wine for about six months. I felt sorry for this girl with such a prolific psychological trigger, but not too sorry. The daughters of whiskey drunks know better than to hitch all their baggage to Jim Beam.

VOLPERT

New York is a bloodbath

In another world, perhaps we are our same selves doing something else we'd rather be doing, but every world is still perfect. Put two fires together & they make a bigger fire, but two icebergs put together breed a little awkward carnage & then they begin to melt. We are vigilant while our boots make parentheticals in the puddle achieved by freedom of choice & that's what grace means. Hell is other people, on one condition. You have to believe that you're either holding the gun, or you're under it. In our deeper hearts, I suspect each of us knows what we could & cannot have.

VOLPERT

Adults are children
like weapons are tools

Uncle Saul had to pick me up from preschool & one day told me I was beginning to grow a monkey tail. The next week, he said it looked longer. I confess I did a shoulder check, but he said only grown ups could see it. Aunt Fran corroborated & I commenced freaking out. This is partly why it took me awhile to come out of the closet. Twenty years later, we were sitting shiva for my grandmother. On day three, I stuck a finger in Saul's back & told him he was beginning to grow a monkey tail. He had no idea what I was talking about.

VOLPERT

I have two vampire hands

They are gypsy piano player slender with sharp scissor nails. People will say lesbians don't like this. What's good is the arch of a palm acquainted with throttle grips, the flurry of digits accustomed to occupying an imagination. My grandmother had these hands, gold chains cascading down both wrists while cursing. Couldn't read a lick of Hebrew, but was as superstitious as they come. Family tree branches went into the chipper of world war while she dwelt on a girl who disappeared into the thicket. We are Transylvanian Jews & I did not tell my grandmother I was queer before she died, because I am quite sure she knew.

VOLPERT

You can't just follow your nose

The first perfume I fell in love with was called Happy, worn by an overweight depressive who I treated well until the abusive ex came to claim what was hers. Businesswomen on the train are still temporarily mesmerized when I lean in & tell them what they are wearing. I can smell that & a cologne called Curve at twenty yards. Curve was an alcoholic & a good friend who said we couldn't date because I wasn't domesticated. When my wife & I met, she got itchy or sneezy from most scents & I smelled like a pillar of salt at rest under stage lights.

Adventure is nice

Maybe we are going to the grocery store, but just maybe we are eloping to Mexico. After all this time, the wife still surprises me. I keep my tank at least half full, in case she asks me to go to the moon. But we find romance like loose change in the couch cushions & I don't understand people who save up for years just to spend one week in Paris. Wherever life takes us, I hope there's a Waffle House. That's the only place you can still count on getting 2% milk without specifically asking for it & the wife doesn't like me to order it.

VOLPERT

Some people look at the stars

Business travel is deeply boring & I always miss my wife so much if she can't come with me. Sometimes I'm expected to hit up a hot spot, but when left alone, I head down to the hotel restaurant. There's no shortage of steaks, but if it's a Tuesday, I go for the spaghetti. The wife & I have spaghetti most Tuesdays, & I just want to feel close to her by doing what we would do at home. As far as sauce goes, my wife's is the best, even if it just comes out of a different jar from the very same company the restaurant uses.

VOLPERT

The stomach is a window to the soul

My wife tells this great story about a girl she knew who turned vegan after having what she described as a soulful connection with a chicken. She was driving behind a truck with feathers flying everywhere & made eye contact with one of the birds. Even though I count a fair number of whack jobs among my better friends, I just couldn't hang out with a person like that. For about five years, I tried pretty hard to be a vegetarian. For the most part, I've never made it further than the ethical problem of responsibility for killing more chickens by ordering the all-drumstick bucket.

VOLPERT

A fruit is a fountain

The first time I ate an apple fritter it was so good it was practically imaginary. There was a phase where nothing would do for breakfast besides apple fritters. The aroma of fry bread still calls up an animalistic longing for sticky fingers of times past. Now, life is a dream where my wife's insides are covered with strawberry seeds I want to get stuck in my teeth. Everybody thinks it's all about the juice, but really people are hungry for something that lasts awhile. A friend once told me pears are devastating because after your first excellent pear, you'll spend forever in quest of another.

VOLPERT

It's never the same zoo twice

I found my favorite window when I was about five. There was a phony rock formation, then some steps going down. It was a huge plate of glass, beyond which was a vast turquoise shine of water. But I waited a long time in the shadows there, perching half my little butt on the ledge of that window until the splash came. A polar bear's front paws pushed off the glass inches from my nose while every long white hair on its massive body waved at me. Went back there when I turned thirty, but waited for nothing. Had to be content watching a seal show from the bleachers.

VOLPERT

Ankles disappear

They used to go behind my head. There were bony knobs that would cut cleanly through glassine pools, step out soulfully tanned & ready to run. Now my shoes feel too tight. Those delicate corners have been rounded by the fat of a career & a few too many loose cobblestone sprains. I wonder when I will be able to predict a storm is coming & want to define living daylights. Attempt to circumnavigate the space of things that have been scared out of you & try to tie a rope around all those things of which you used to be so certain. Use a mirror to do it.

VOLPERT

No bonus for backs broken

The thing about rock & roll is that you're in really good shape, until you're not. Then you can either acquiesce to letting people feel sorry for you for aging, as mortal coils are wont to do, or devote yourself to more charitable endeavors like funding Fender Strats for twelve year olds. I sometimes forget that it's a bad idea to stage dive when entertaining an audience full of rich people. Don't even chance it metaphorically, because they won't get it & hand you instead a needless let down. Just sweat through your worn black t-shirt & keep the lights out of your eyes.

VOLPERT

Yeah means yeah

I didn't go to prom & I didn't screw anybody in a frat house. I haven't killed anything that crossed the road in front of me. I only order the smallest cup of coffee & I never pay extra for extra cilantro. A willingness to wear wrinkled clothing has changed my life for the better. Ninety percent of the time I am touching my bike, I have gloves on. Whatever my father's failings, liking country music is not among them. Everybody has to have rules, but only some people make exceptions & those are the ones who naturally expect you to bend your rules on their behalf.

VOLPERT

I am reluctant to get a dog

There's a certain type of dog that sees a bike from the lawn & starts to give chase, even though to catch me means to get killed. I slow down when approaching the definition of animal instinct, then speed quickly past the point of interception. The other dog has its tongue lolling out, out the window. This dog & I are friends. Sometimes I dream about buying this dog a sidecar, but a bike isn't a bike if it has more than two wheels. You can't really tell which kind of animal you have until you get it home for a while & see, & I'm not the type that returns a dog.

Don't ride the mechanical bull

I think I am better than most people in many ways & people who prefer to carry on believing such a thing about themselves should not attempt to solve trigonometry equations in a honky tonk bar. There must be a right place & a right time to show your work. Meanwhile, Mount Everest is just crawling with desperate hyperventilators looking to prove their worth to the most stoic pinnacle of rock formations. It's tempting to work on the wine instead of simply eating the grapes, but after you've had a few good glasses, the fateful moment arrives where you expect the saddle will buck predictably just for special you.

Keep cracked glasses
& chipped plates

There were days when nothing but the sound of solid things shattering would do. Sometimes I offered part of my stash of slightly broken dishes to grieving friends & they always looked at me like I was nuts. But a deep frustration that hurls pottery against the concrete floor of a carport is not the thing to bottle up in shame. Few things released me like the sound of breaking glass. Nobody ever called the cops on me for it. I once even saw our neighbor watching me from her second story window. She waved & smiled. I swept up & the daylight felt broad.

VOLPERT

The hair has stopped falling out

Deliberating over then declaring this was an exercise in a gray area. Probably I shuddered at making the call that scheduled the appointment that resulted in diagnosis. Certainly I fell down wormholes of chronic pain & crossed minefields to sign the treaty that accepted this disease. Wear my intestines on my sleeve & they will bleed all over you. But it was just water, rising around me in the shower when the simple remnants of my vanity would not let it pass, which finally broke me. We do not ever refer to these tiny nets of sanity as clumps. I look terrible in hats, but rather cool in a helmet.

VOLPERT

These are the fruits
of incurable illness

People say that if you don't have your health, you don't have anything. But bodies fail, by design. Having a drink on the 96th floor has nothing to do with looking down on a dizzying view of the city. I was diagnosed, there for an unobstructed view of the sky. We didn't take any photos. My mother used to put out huge platters of fruit for us to pick at after school. We grabbed & ran. But the other day, I ate an overripe black plum so perfect it brought tears to my eyes, the ghosts of Christina Rossetti & William Carlos Williams breathing down my neck.

VOLPERT

That t-shirt has my name on it

There is a girl in the front row that drove five hours to wait three more in the cold, listening exclusively to my albums for the entire eight hours. She was in Chicago last night. Please, sweetheart, go home. I'm just not that interesting. In truth, I'm more than a little tired, but we booked this gig nine months ago & everybody has to make a living. I can see her misting up in the spotlights. She doesn't care that there's no encore. She is going to spend another hour behind the theater, shivering near a door out of which I never come. But maybe one time, I will.

There's a difference between
familiar & recurring

It was in a store full of ominous things, this giant butcher knife painted with orange flames & a googly-eyed cartoon face. It was some kind of sick sculpture & the knife was holding an equally large gun in its silly Mickey Mouse hands. Both gun part & knife part appeared to be in working order, a surreal weaponry combo meant to aid me in disemboweling myself. When I have chronic pain at night, this is the kind of ugly thing my unconscious will often produce. I always wake up before the part where I get into the bathtub, but that part is nevertheless implied.

VOLPERT

I never wake up screaming

ONLY RIDE

This is because the pain is not sudden. My body does not consider it to be news. It is more like letting your pet sleep in the bed, even though you know it intensely dislikes you. Even as it depends on you & has no voice except the one you imagine for it, you give in to it enough to let it patrol along the edge of your turf. When its little paw jabs me in the stomach, this isn't a surprise, but another volley in the slim conversation between my stoic part & my animal part in which no decisive victory is ever declared except by death.

VOLPERT

Don't chase the white whale

Death is shoeless horse hooves. We are an engine turning over in winter, grasping for solutions. I don't know any Irish drinking songs, but my entire body can turn still with reckoning when I catch such a melody on the wind. It seems like every time the candle goes out, there are reasons to light a fresh one. I once almost puked during an IMAX movie about deep-sea creatures & not for the proportions of the picture. I couldn't stand the close-ups of their eyes. It's true that what doesn't kill you makes you stronger, just not until it's done scaring the holy hell out of you.

VOLPERT

I miss my dead dog

She died of an aneurysm just before her second birthday, which would have been on the eleventh of September. So she was born under a bad sign & was a fairly bad dog, though loyal as all hell. We didn't know each other too well, but we were pretty comfortable & clearly planned to spend the next ten years or so together. Now I have this ghost dog that I don't need to run home & feed, which is nice. She takes naps on my chest that don't keep me warm. I guess death haunts you down, or I'm not the type that forgets a dog.

VOLPERT

Killing ten minutes is murder

I miss cigarettes every day, but they are expensive & bad for your health. My buddy, who died of a brain tumor, smoked right up until the end. That's fair. Short of accidentally stepping in front of a bus, she knew how she was going & it wasn't tobacco. Sometimes it took ten minutes for her to communicate she wanted a smoke, then somebody had to wheel her outside & so on. I admire the hell out of that. She wasn't wasting any time. A few folks light up each year to commemorate her death, but I can't. I'm an addict.

VOLPERT

Religion is in the mail

There have been a dozen bar mitzvahs, weddings & funerals. I have never set foot in a house of worship uninvited & never lived in a house with high ceilings. My wife will not get a tattoo because she wants to be buried in a Jewish cemetery. My mother-in-law plucked her eyebrows into oblivion & then tattooed them back on. She's also never been drunk, whereas I once drank two forties of King Cobra every night for seventy days. When I say I will be cremated because I am afraid of zombies, people laugh as if I am kidding, but the body is the temple.

VOLPERT

A place without work
is no heaven to me

ONLY RIDE

Sometimes during orgasm I see the faces of dead friends. They are waving & smiling with laughter from up & across, happy I have checked in by flinging a moment of condensed purity over the wall between us. I believe they are working as much as I am, finishing business & settling their accounts. Glad as I am to see them, sometimes one of these faces disappears where I can't get it back again & I celebrate that they have found enough peace to get recycled. Whatever the methods, a soul is the part of humanity that is a perpetual motion machine.

VOLPERT

Viva Las Vegas

I like death as going off-stage. That's pretty. My kid sister worked lights for the plays in high school & sometimes I would sit off-stage up in the rafters with her. So, I have been to death. When my sister & I last hung out, I told her tell them I love them when you go home & tell them I'm never coming home. She didn't believe me, so I sweetened the deal. I put cherries on top of my pretty please. I told her I loved her in sign language. It's the horns, which is also the hand gesture that means rock & roll.

VOLPERT

I recommend the Zebra Lounge

If I had a dollar for every time I've cried in a hole in the wall piano bar, I'd have sixty-five dollars. If I had a dollar for every time I've been drunk at a hole in the wall piano bar, I'd only have forty dollars. This is why I haven't been to a karaoke bar since college. Karaoke bars are for losers, whereas piano bars are for the lost. So I have often had occasion to praise the sweetness of Caroline or demand the piano man sing us a song. Everybody should sometimes yell real loud & cry a little. It's cheaper than beer.

VOLPERT

Say what you will when I am gone

Speak ill of the dead because they are already being reborn & preparing to speak ill of you. The light bulb above my head is not broken. I've unscrewed it slightly so that you have a false sense of security about its accuracy as an indicator of my genius & I can meanwhile go on thinking whatever I please. Everyone I admire is distilling into Tom Waits or Patti Smith. Let me finish this thought, because it might not be here when I get back. I aspire to have been not the poet laureate of rock & roll, but the rock & roll laureate of poetry.

VOLPERT

I almost failed statistics

I do know the chance of life over death is fifty-fifty each day. My life has been going on for a while, but length of life does not much touch one's closeness to death. Sometimes I douse myself with humility & then strike a match. While I am on fire, I think about how hard it is & how important it is not to scream. Everybody is on fire & everybody can see it, so screaming doesn't add anything to our situation. Maybe one's years do not even connect to one's experience of life. I am thinking about the Dalai Lama, a child & a ghost at the same time.

VOLPERT

Whitman lives

I work with someone whose friend has an autistic son. When she needs alone time, she sends him out into the backyard with scissors. He will sit down & cut a few leaves of grass at a time, for hours. He really enjoys it. My coworker is laughing as she tells me about this, but she is smiling like it is incredible & she is judging her friend for it. Somebody is a bad mother. I want to know what they do with all those little clippings, but I don't want to ask & be judged. I would send the kid out to the front lawn.

VOLPERT

I have superior night vision

Four in the morning is the hour of the wolf. That's when my alarm clock goes off, just like Ben Franklin's. The stillest hour before dawn is a space for contemplation, even in my younger years when it was after closing time & late night breakfast. I have always loved campus most when it is empty. People do hideous things under the cover of daylight, but in the clear cold quiet broken only by my seventy miles per hour, any animal awake is my friend. The abyss yawns & stretches before us, intelligent & unprepared to negotiate.

VOLPERT

Coming down is the hardest thing

ONLY RIDE

For several years now, I have seen the sunrise every weekday. My primary instinct is to splash in it like a puddle, to clamber up into the abstract & two-dimensional ceiling of reality with vaguely criminal intentions. Like most people, my first time flying was a Disney trip. I remember the sky better than the theme park. My mother was at a loss because I asked whether we could see my dead bunny rabbit from up there. Everybody was looking down at the tiny, teeming metropolis, which I thought was dumb. So I peered out & across, trying to bridge infinity with little more than my unsharpened imagination.

VOLPERT

Hunter Thompson is sugar-free

He calls at four to bark & mutter concerning black tongue, about which I know nothing except that I am awake. The cell battery increasingly beeps & finally dies, then the man is dead, just as I approach vision focus purpose readiness openness to the energy of greater something. In the classroom like it is still all good, my students want a clear definition of transcendentalism. I pull it together too slowly until they are freaked into wondering what will be on the test, except for the stoned kid in the corner who asks what Owl Farm is. The earth immediately resumes rotation because I am sharing airspace with this kid.

VOLPERT

This is brown bear soup

That's what my little brother said at age three, when our grandfather asked him why he was battering an empty bowl with a wooden spoon. My brother & I grew up in the same house, but I didn't know I didn't know him until I watched him huff a Sharpie to get high in rehab. He is wanted for felonies in two states, but he managed to get his GED first. I teach like I am on one of those cop shows where a hardcase joins the force to avenge the fact that his sister was abducted when they were kids. If only I'd been a little more vigilant & needling blame games like that.

VOLPERT

We see something terrible
& bloom

Look at the sky, so you know what the emergency is. Fires happen at night. Floods happen during the day. Every natural disaster wants to perform when it can be best seen. There is this special type of black mold that only grows where there has been a flood. It's toxic. But there is also a mushroom, a black morel, which only grows where there has been a fire. It's delicious. The event is not really the thing, just a seed. In museums, I probably spend sixty percent of the time looking at people looking & just forty percent looking at what they're looking at.

VOLPERT

The priest & the punk wear black

When you naturally get older, or even when you're young but something pretty deadly serious happens to you, either you find religion or you find rock & roll. One comes with a book & the other comes with a bike. For the most part, the book people & the bike people think each other are a little crazy. Inside though, we all know everybody's grave is the same number of feet deep & most people put their pants on one leg at a time. There's not much else that needs to be nailed down, but then, I'm just one of those bike people.

VOLPERT

You are suspended

ONLY RIDE

When I was a kid, nobody I knew was out of the closet. Actually, I didn't know anybody who was in the closet either. There were rumors about an English teacher that made her my favorite, but then other rumors about why I was her favorite. Some people become the thing they try to escape & others become the thing that saves them. Ducking & covering across the many barriers to my certification, I conjure before you the only openly queer faculty member in this public Southern high school, fully equipped to teach both English & tolerance. You are failing tolerance & that's why I wrote you up. You're welcome.

VOLPERT

The train is two minutes late

Nobody on the platform can do anything about it, so they are making sympathetic grumpy faces at each other & shifting impatiently from foot to foot. As a consequence, more than half of the people on the train will miss their transfer. This costs each of those crabby people an additional thirteen to twenty-eight minutes. I am one of these people, arriving at work to find one of my students leading her class through the beginning of my lesson plan. This is the day she starts imagining herself as a teacher. That's what delay is about, the timing of our connections.

VOLPERT

Filthy lucre never sleeps

If I see a penny on the ground, I leave it there thinking somebody surely needs it more than I do. Some people pick them up only if they're heads or tails, but that's pure superstition. The other day I found a rolled up twenty in the hallway at work & grabbed it. Bad karmic backlash for depriving a careless student of weekly drug money quickly ensued & the rest of the day was one lame setback after another. To cheer up, I checked in on one of my favorite musicians. He's coming to town on Friday & bingo, tickets cost me twenty bucks.

VOLPERT

Gather your comforts

I pretty much have the kind of problems that a pot of macaroni & cheese can solve, except that a lot of people think I think about death a little too often. These are white, suburban problems. I know that. Let's make fun of me for not saying more about children who are starving & carrying assault rifles. I deserve it, unless a spider crawls up over the round of your delicate shoulder & suddenly distracts you from your own more selfless concerns. This is why I want a dog. When the moment finally comes, I won't be the only one to hear the fly buzz.

VOLPERT

This is my post now

It used to be that whenever you were at a loss, you could retreat to the public park around the corner. Or later, you could step aside & light up a smoke. Those places are gone. I flick the pollen off my bike while the neighborhood stray cat eyes me with suspicion. An old woman I don't know waves at me as she jogs past. So much of living is listening quietly for signs that the guardians of decorum have fallen asleep at their posts. A kid walks by, eyes on his feet like he is doing nothing wrong. We have the same shoes on.

VOLPERT

There need not be fire
where there's smoke

I might like to get up early in the morning & coat an otherwise blank dewy air current with the great good scent of kick starting BBQ smokers. It could waft briskly across all our weekend expectations, canceling the modern fury of time & its accompanying dread of quietude. The sting & the salt of it would warm the marrow of everyone who has grown tired of waiting for something. No more spark & no more thunderbolt, no more explosive unrest, just the purple haze of our everlasting cooking & some water in the eye for hickory or apple wood reasons.

VOLPERT

It's too close to call

Keep pushing til it's understood. Let five o'clock shadows alight on the eye's lower lids. Go out over the line. We're open all night. By turns, be tired & be the answers. If it must brake, keep something incessant inside to remember where everything left off. Let the past burn & keep that smoke in the pocket of an everyday jacket. Be glad you're alive. Eat something. Look east & west. I don't believe the thrill is all gone. No matter what we think it's about, living will have been only a little about what we think it's about.

VOLPERT

I have no goat to get

Many things annoy me, but I am seldom really angry because now I just feel so lucky to be alive. If that sounds cliché, you are still among the people who don't know how lucky living is. Just admit it. Death knocks twice: once for introductions & once to take you away. I gave my goat to death. Now I am back at work. You stay here & complain about how your dad was an asshole. Sit right there until your hip hurts & you realize your shadow on the lawn has given ground to twilight. I'll be driving a bike headed into the thick.

VOLPERT

Ride like the Dickinson

Because no one should stop for death, it rides alongside me. The sidecar holds but just itself, my own mortality. I throttle hard. I make great haste & will not put away my labor or my leisure, views of our civility. We passed the school, my students grown & distant in their things. We passed the fields of blazing pain & snaked the river run. I braked in front of lights that were well guarded by its hounds, their sparkle barely visible & silence all around. Since then it's many moons & each is longer than that day, that first surprise. The bike's headlight rode toward eternity.

VOLPERT

A Note on the Text

The fonts used in this publication are:

DEATH RATTLE BB
Open Sans

Acknowledgments

The editors of these fine journals first published some form of the work that appears in this book, for which I am grateful: *2River View, Airplane Reading, Barefoot Review, Boog City, Clementine Magazine, Coconut, Dead Mule School of Southern Literature, Dressing Room Poetry Journal, eratio, Esque, Prose-Poem Project, Pure Francis, RHINO, Sleet Magazine, Stone Highway Review, Sweet, Tattooed Poets Project.* Thanks also to those editors who sought fit to anthologize some of these pieces: Julie R. Enszer in *Milk & Honey*, Kodac Harrison & Collin Kelley in *Java Monkey Speaks*, and Kevin Simmonds in *Collective Brightness.*

Photograph by Rob Friedman

About the Author

MEGAN VOLPERT is the author of five books on communication and popular culture, most notably about Andy Warhol. She is also editor of *This assignment is so gay: LGBTIQ Poets on the Art of Teaching.* For the better part of a decade, Volpert has been doing three things: teaching high school English in Atlanta, living with ulcerative colitis, and driving a motorcycle. Predictably, her website is www.meganvolpert.com.

About the Press

Founded in 2010, SIBLING RIVALRY PRESS is an independent publishing house based in Alexander, Arkansas. Our mission is to publish work that disturbs and enraptures. Also predictably, our website is www.siblingrivalrypress.com.